Mayada Himani is a Lebanese – British citizen. She started out her career in the media as a presenter with Middle East Broadcasting Centre in London. She currently lives between London and Beirut, where her story with blue began to take shape. Most pictures were taken on the Lebanese coast, where the mercurial blue sea, allowed Mayada to connect to a more spiritual world. Her work is an intuitive exploration of the smallest detail we pass everyday on the streets and tend to ignore. "My story with Blue" measures our daily sentiments in our smallest steps and translates them into words.

For Samir

And
all those
who believe in Angels

Mayada Himani

My Story with Blue

To kiki,

The beautiful Empath, smart, helpful, huminatarian patron to the minds. The list is endless.

Thank you for being so special.

love

Mayada

AUSTIN MACAULEY PUBLISHERS™
LONDON * CAMBRIDGE * NEW YORK * SHARJAH

A CIP catalogue record for this title is available from the British Library.

ISBN 9781528977982 (Paperback)
ISBN 9781528977999 (Hardback)
ISBN 9781528978019 (ePub e-book)

www.austinmacauley.com

First Published (2021)
Austin Macauley Publishers Ltd
25 Canada Square
Canary Wharf
London
E14 5LQ

Grateful to my husband and sons, Jad and Ziyad Mourad, who didn't shy away from my writing but rather encouraged it. Special thanks to my childhood friend, Wafa Huballah, who bought and carried by hand across many seas my first professional camera. To Raya who waited patiently for me to click the button on our morning power walks. To my beautiful sisters and brothers, my pillars in life. To my mum, an angel on Earth. To Mia Baraka and Ibrahim Kombarji who transformed my initial postcard photos into a book. There are so many people close to my heart that I would like to mention without making the process mute for the reader. The pictures and words in this book are dedicated to all of them. Complete happiness doesn't come without my nephews, nieces, cousins and in-laws. To the readers: Never let a moment pass. Follow your imagination.

Few Words by the Artist

Inside the circle of the sun and the moon and this small window, that's where my story lies, my story with blue. The Earth holds my present and the rest of the planets I can see hold my future lives. Nothing is alien to me. In this life, I am a human spirit. We all take turns to become stars and light the sky. I was lucky enough to come across many stars who continue to shine their light on me: family and friends. My story with blue is my story with the sea, my story with the letter S.

S Impacts My Life,

Sons, Sheltered School…Scorching Sun… Sand…Solace and Silence…Heart-warming Smiles, Summer breeze and Solid friendships. Sound Siblings, a Sea of love; Samir, Samar, Sawsan, and Samer. I Sense and appreciate Sensibility, Sensuality, and Sexuality. I am a Sensitive Scorpio and a Snake with no Slur. I Stand Strong like a Samurai and Sit like a Supple S. Away from Spotlights… Soul-Searching…Superstitions…Submission to God…Sense of Security…Sky Sprinkling water for Spring…Snow…I Sprint to my Sizable fridge…Surprise! It starts with an S… Sub- zero.

Sugar!

Sincerely, Mayada

My Story with Blue

An end without a beginning behind the smiles untold stories Some shining, some haunting, Like the infinite swift currents Memories spinning and dulling Serving as a temporary divergent
For nothing is certain.

Sacred Friendship

My heart is transparent You crown my space
Pierce my thoughts, breathe words into me and then take flight
Your soul beams wide, so I take the spiral slide Not for the adventure,
but for the light
Travel beckons, we reunite
Travel beckons again, we lose touch You live through consciousness
I live absorbed through emotion, is that wrong? One day you will
understand
You are my guide I am your friend

We are one.

A Blue Day

I can picture the surrounding I see you on the beach
And then my eyes shut.

I pick up the image again of the Calm blue sea…
    the white-hot sand
Children at play…
Your silhouette and my mind stops.

I can't move forward
I can't breathe underwater

I am stuck in my imagination

Too Beautiful to Face...

I think you just wanted vast space Put on your running shoes, it's okay
Don't go far, don't ask why, don't leave me dry
I have too many questions of my own

Is beauty not divine?

In our assertiveness for God
We stumble on beauty and love,
Or we stumble on the beauty of love to realize God?

What is the ultimate quest?
To find someone that gratifies the quench I am on my fourth limb
This cannot be the end.

I Want to Follow the Arrow Across the Sea

And meet you at the other end. Will you be there?

Underworld

You want to kiss? What if it's pure bliss?
It's better to give it a miss
So we stay clear of the abyss.

Come closer Feel my words

I don't need to make a sound when my heart pounds It beats faster to your words

While you speak of a kiss I am living the kiss… Imagining your lips Continue talking…

I have to remember to breathe

Don't interrupt my scene by asking me to speak Hold my hand, imagine it with me

Be comfortable in my silence.

Where Do I Go from Here?

Colorful bars obstruct my vision Are they from my end or yours?
All the paint I inhale spells your name, Caught between the bold red and
precious blue I am torn inside,
The fabric of my time on a canvas,
I feel timid

Bring back your paintbrush,
Draw our memory of love,
No dark colors, no dark times, just rainbows
It's time to make decisions
Be wise, my soul; it's not too late, Keep your mending heart safe.

Infinites

I thought your heart was shaped by blue A hundred glitter points of possibilities Creation meeting realization
Just a thought that remained at the distant sea.

Building Blocks

Your wall is made of clear glass Mine is made of bricks
Where there is a gap There is a barbed wire
And a moral compass with a guilty conscience It feels like a trap
Especially when there is so much to admire And more to desire.

I Am Living in My Shadow

Wishing I was in a meadow Full of flowers and trees
But I am a slave to my circumstances I have had no chances
I face my shadow every day Asking me how long will I stay?
But I have no answers
So I say, let's just play.

Nostalgia

I want the Nostos without the Algos I want to return without the
suffering
I have no mottos, just happy moments

    on loan…
    until I'm shown
    how to be at home with your moan.

A Choice in Flames

Let your light seep into my skin Let it lead me to the truth
Truth of our sincerity Of our friendship
Of our innocent bond To hold you forever
To comfort your fears So I can be at ease
Let your light shine on my face See my eyes
They go deep beyond your gaze See my eyes
Feel my sorrow... Share my joy They go beyond my understanding...
Beyond my skin...
Beyond your gaze...beyond your light.

Many Hearts Were Broken

With utterances unspoken Growing up I needed to do To open up and chew...
It wasn't intentional, you know It's not my fault, I used to say It's my ego playing away...

My other self wanted the esteem And therefore, enjoyed the steam... So in my defence
I put up a fence...
And now that I am older My heart is softer...
   it has been broken Game over.

Roadblocks

I tried to recall the touch of your hand
And I couldn't,
I closed my eyes harder And I imagined your grip But it slipped
Even my brain tugged
Couldn't revisit the hug
I want to fantasize about our snug Would that cause a real disorder?

I See Myself

Putting prayers on the shelf It's a thing I do
When I'm so confused
Because I reject all the abuse from this world.

Too Much Blue

Yesterday I hoped for tomorrow
Today I live in sorrow Yesterday it was you
Today it is you
Years from now, it will still be you
    it has always been you.

Let's Empty Our Hearts

And begin the journey over again.

Snakes and Ladders

I thought I was too grown up to fall in love Too wise for this parasite
and the hurt as its price

But then you came along… A feeling of pleasure arose
I climbed the ladder to smell the rose

Now I wait for your embrace
Sick and tired of the snakes

Time has never gone this slow Although it is in motion

I know.

Sunset

My feet ache Tired of the search
I just want to rest…in the hot sand
   and watch the sunset.

Take Your Time

Why does the turtle walk so slow
   is it because of a heavy heartload

Maybe it likes to take its time To absorb all that has gone by Maybe this
is the flow…
And we all need to go slow…
   to be in the know…

                                        I don't want to go.

Cover My Back

While I bathe in blue
Kiss me where it aches as my heart breaks I gamble my fate
   not knowing how much longer I must wait

Let me see your naked face My neck hurts
Please move to my left so I can shield you
Don't be troubled…keep the faith…peace to you.

A Mellow Whisper

I thought I heard the trees calling your name
    they must feel the flame...

I Touched His Essence

Becoming an adolescent I often wondered why
Now I wonder how it all began I really don't know
But it's beginning to show
All the things I need to outgrow

Let's swim in everything that's blue and be children again.

In Solitude

My dreams come true
I put my feet up and imagine you.

Two-Halves

I love the person you are
I whispered it in your left ear Did you hear? Maybe not
Your hands were holding me tight And I no longer knew who I was

I promised you protection
But what about the strong connection I feel so light
I have no fear I feel hot
Hold me again…tight and tighter
Until our forms become one.

Living with Memories

I dreamt you came back We took the empty boats
And filled them with kisses and laughter

Adrift

I feel like I am in a cloud
The voice in my head is so loud
Can you hold my head between both your hands… Like you usually do
Slow down my racing heartbeat
I'm over eighteen, running on caffeine My naked body hides under a
shroud Wanting to make you proud.

I Am in Pieces

God keeps me connected by showing me colors Of things I can sense
Beauty I can touch
My faith then increases My trust absolute… My palette electric
My life accepted.

I Took a Walk

By the water
I found my chakra in an orange ball Tossed in the sea
Floating away from me.

I Believe in Magic

I looked for signs to find you, In the process, I found me.

Is the image I have of you
Different to the reality of you?

Like a fool, I will dive into your blueness with my head first

Half a Century to Find You

Under the gaze of blue

The path ahead looked complicated
One foot forward, one thought backward I came to you unabashed,
feelings true You turned me away,
The me you know so well but cannot sense Look beyond yourself, make
amends,
The moment has gone Yet I remain by your side.

I Was Born an Adult

Choked up with grief Wanting this life to be brief Far removed from the cult

Unable to heal my wounds without insult – injury to others Lost in my purposeless responsibilities of pleasing

Now I am choked up with gratitude

The beauty you speak of, only you can touch God is great.

I Want

I want the rain to wash my sins My regrets in a bin
Start new in a color of blue.

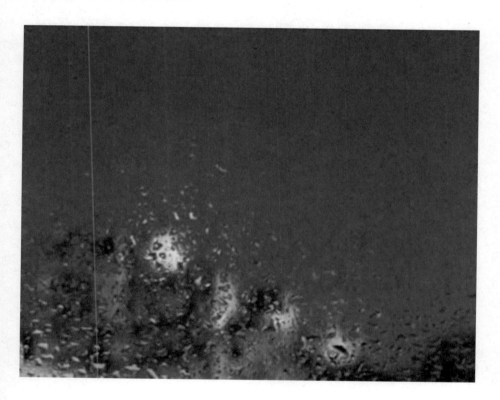

Will We Meet?

I Am Confused

The choice is not mine to make Whatever color I choose
It leads to blue A symbol of you
I can no longer equate which path to take.

Balance

My friend says it's all about acceptance I doubt it's without repentance

I see God
With a glass of champagne Toasting away the pain And who do we blame?
We are always reminded of Cain

But are we able to live without a bloodstain?

Sunrise

Sunset, Sunlight, Sunrise, Orange, Moonlight, Sunset, Moonlight, Blue,

Then the Earth conspired
     that we should meet,

Sunlight Sunset
So we can tweet… Sunrise
Sunset
Of all things sweet Sunrise
Sunset

Take a seat
Stay on my right…

Sunrise
Twilight
Starlight.

                              and tell me about your highlights

A Glimpse of a Search

A walk through reality
I thought we were on the same stretch painfully
    innocently fused together

While I trusted the energy that directs you,
You knocked me over with a feather.

Exit

The color blue is slowly disappearing beneath the white
Time has phased out the intense moments No longer deep, nor profound
The soul that cannot be tied
    Misty, Mystic, Elusive blue…

Why

I looked up at the sky for mercy
    everything I touch is infused with pain

I don't want to suffer much longer
I want to fly the sky, leave the city

The flicker of endless light is growing
It's the evangelic spirits calling my name,
I want to return

    eternal love
    eternal peace please don't grieve

I have arrived safely.

Obituary

My spirit trusted your spirit, a delight My soul, your soul, did you not say "I am you"?

I am not you
I found myself in you
I am myself deep within you And deep within
There is enough light in me For I follow the sun
And worship the universe that gave me life

And you, like death Are no longer relevant.

When I Am Alone

I turn to the stone
I trace the time on their lines

What I find sometimes is very sublime
And sometimes, it's not worth a dime.

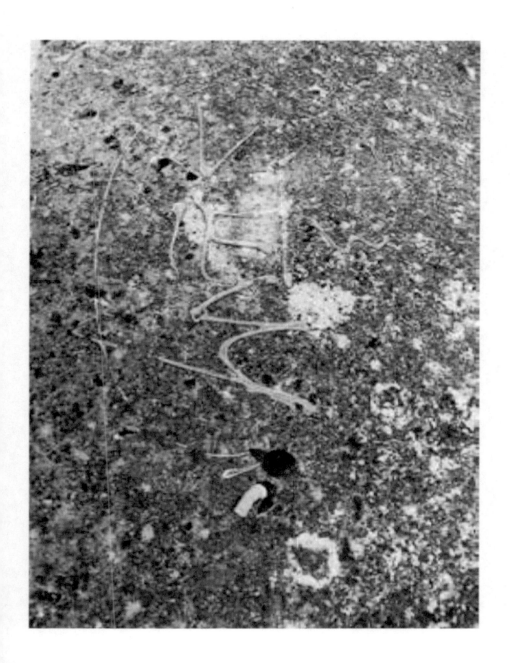

You Took Me Somewhere I Did Not Want to Go

I was still making love to you when you left
I wanted to admire and kiss every inch of your body I thought I had time.

With you I am whole…I am me… I search no more
I was lost and now I am lost inside you My dreams are altered
I do not want to sleep, lest you leave
You didn't give me a chance to turn the page
Why did you read me the ending before the beginning? I saw you leave,
I had to let you go
I anticipated your goodbye
You are a bird with wings of an eagle Take the book with you
It's over 88 pages long, weighs a tonne
     I cannot carry it alone

It's all about special you from beginning to end
I still feel your heartbeat pressed against my chest

                              I felt you coming way before we met.

Graffiti

Grown from a wounded soul
The writing was on a Parisian wall Yet I took the fall
While you remained standing tall
    how does your wall remain tainted free?

Forgive Me, I Had to Leave

Sometimes God Answers

He sends you a gift and puts it at your doorstep But you mistake it for a
test
It's not a test, it's something else:

An elevator ride
If you are only in search of the light A reincarnated friend from the past
Or a past lover from a wasted life
Knock, knock...I wish I can open the door This is the raw truth:
I can now see my colors
Knock knock...
I am the recipient of your light.

Let's Smoke a Cigarette

I want to be the flame on your lips So I can pause your kiss
I want to be the love you inhale And the thought you exhale
I want to be your cigarette
And go with you to the highest minaret Why are you looking so pale?
Let your lips touch my tits Put your legs around my hips Do you feel any
better?

Let's smoke a cigarette.

I Have Formed a Coloured Picture of You

It comes not from knowing you But from reading you
Maybe I don't understand What it is you command

        or maybe you are meant to be read in black and white!

Amber scents

If I had the courage to speak to you
I would say mountains in the language of wind and flower I would speak
words fluid as water
I would be the tree you lean on
Shield you from sorrow with my leaves till they fall
          over concrete walls,

Our predestined acts are not our own Do you not trust the call?
Come close, smell the amber
          touch my speaking skin,

For time has still not given me the courage to speak.

Half Man

A whiff of Heaven A breath of air
Air is man on number eleven Moisture is woman…
But she remains forbidden Head of a God
As he flies the sky like a bird skidding Sky is another woman.

Air Force Blue

Baby blue, Cobalt blue… Electric blue, Midnight blue… Royal blue,
Sky blue, Steel blue…
So many shades of blue. Which one are you?
How do I find you?

He Expressed a Sound:

Hmmm

And I imagined making love to him endlessly It was better than words.

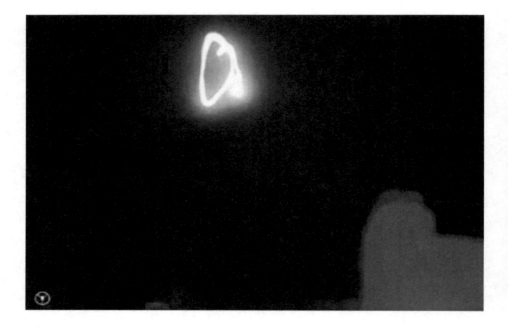

I Am Not Walking Away, Just Shy

I need time before you draw the curtains I want to look out of the
window
    yes, the one on the left

    Show me the self that's yours Everything I see is painted in your
words
    even the birds

Wish I had their wings Where would I go?
    away from here

Let's go back to you... Do you like me in yellow?

There Is Always a Light

Sometimes bright or out of sight Sometimes we miss it
    because we believe it comes from above But it can come from below
From random figures on the road
That trigger a glow and soften the blow.

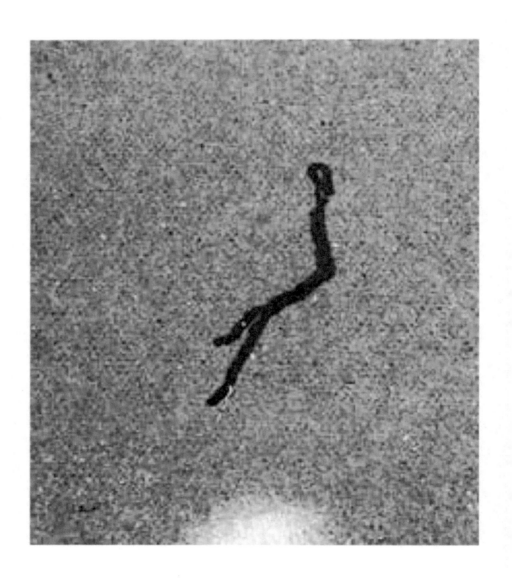

A smile through the sidewalk cracks

Imagination

I draw the tenor of your voice in my head at night
and then I kiss you.

Purity

He surrounds himself with a clear glass wall For all to see
but none to touch

Touch he does people's hearts... With words that turn to dust Dust he
does not fear
For living and dying he holds dear

He surrounds himself with a clear glass wall But I believe it's made of
solid blue gold.

Some Days I Feel Empty and Sad

Others see me beautiful.

Judgement

I lay naked under the mercy of passion But desire showed me no compassion

Then the words began to falter and scrabble
I can't play
I retreated behind my concrete wall
A place where I don't feel small.

Beached

My head tilts to your left I want to meet your stare

Do you still find me pretty in my nudity? Don't look away
Play the guitar
So I can feel comfortable
    with my scars.

False Sense

There were no strings attached only invisible threads
Yet you felt tied and went to hide, Putting me aside in search of yourself
Did you find the self you were looking for?

I found these fallen petals on the road from a fragmented rose.

I Thought Our Bond Was Deep

But you preferred praying your rosary One bead at a time, each
witnessing a lie A different prayer, a different count
One abandoned thought after another

Decades have passed, I am still under your spell
Waiting for sound sleep with your borrowed rosary beads.

Olive Groves by the Beach

Somewhere out of reach
I want to dance in your arms
    to the warmth of your breath.

You Have a Place in My Heart

But my dear, your heart is wild like a nomad's
   restlessly searching for the fertile soon forgotten for a better

You are a hunter, albeit tender
Mile after mile seeking the unknown You don't have to travel far
You have a home in my heart.

All I see is blue even when all there is, is green

Scientifically 60,000 Thoughts a Day

Only one persists today, yesterday and tomorrow

I am now the closest I have been to ruefulness
   and the farthest away from you

Will you write my sorry epitaph when I die?

City Rides

I want to be carried on your bicycle
Feel the wilderness of a blue butterfly
Spark a bonfire with your work
I am in love with the world inside you
To ignore your footprint on my path: impossible

I am jealous
I see the clouds coming
My hands are stiff

Keep me anchored on your moving bicycle.

How I feel… suspended in your kiss.

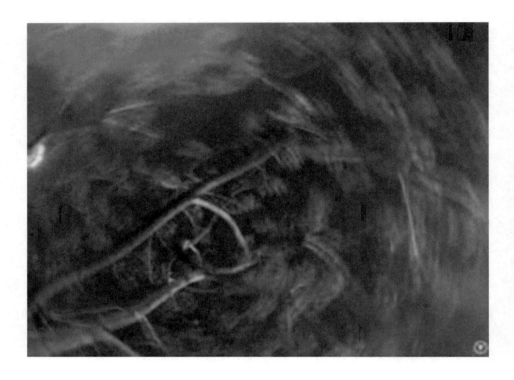

There Is a Bird in My Heart

Can you see it?
It makes my heart flutter And sometimes shutter To be so exposed
I have to be disposed
To the idea of being alone.

It Makes Me Sad

To know that your best times Are when you are alone

Can I be the quiet branch
    at your side?
I will only glance
Without the heartache of a romance.

Before Sadness Sets In

First rays of delight
I open my eyes to thoughts of you

Your spirit, I'm happy inside Your scent fills my lungs
I can taste our journey I draw a deep breath Peace
It's in your color – blue, seismic waves I send you a kiss from side to
side
    above and below

It warms my injured heart
We have endured enough in our parallel lives.

Pockets of Light

The Grass is greener on the distant side It's a life I long for, an illegal prayer

Remain unaware, don't question it now Too much time has elapsed
I have paid dues by wasting my youth
The plants have all shot up
I don't want to plough any longer, it's not negotiable I have planted enough seeds to fill your vacant stare Let it rain, let it cleanse, let it drown
    let it shine

I am ready for all that comes.

I Want to Dance

It's too windy to walk, too cold to swim.

He loves me…
He loves me not… He loves me…

maybe not.

A Trip

I am surrounded by trees and luscious green

By divine creation and colorful fireflies Gratitude fills me
My orange heart centre is empty

I am learning to let you go
    and surprisingly I don't feel low
Are you happy behind your glass wall?

Let's drink some wine and celebrate our nothingness.

Rainbow Time

It's a colorful maze, puts me in a daze I want to explore, but fear to be its prey And I fear wanting more
What if I'm shown the door? That would be a bore, because

I want to explore
And I want to explode in this colorful maze

I just want to hide in a dark cave
And wait for the rainbow.

The voice in my life has no sound
it has a deep echo loud enough to fill your valley.

Thirst

I have been here before And I don't like it
A time long forgotten A scar that never healed
Reminds me why I chose this barren road
The one I fill with color, laughter and everything sweet
    love scares me…
    or maybe I don't know how to love

One last drink if you please
Yes, yes, if you please, one more for the road, this barren road.

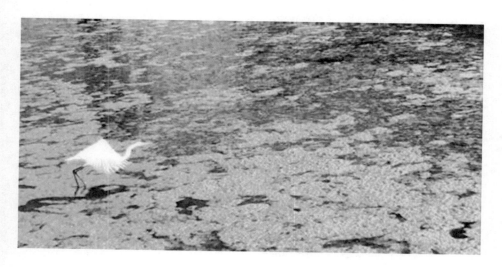

They maimed my body Yet I bloomed…

for beauty grows from within.

Abundance

Those who live in love Live in God
    and God lives in them

Where is your God?
And where does your love reside? Is it still locked up behind the wall?

Let it grow.

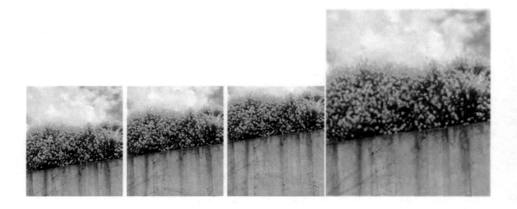

I Am Clear

I am radiant I am whole I am light
I am cold I am hot… I am old… I am dark
I am young

I am all that in a drop, a teardrop And my centre is blue…ice blue.

Compromise of Adam's Apple

You like the yellow
I prefer the taste of green Maybe because you are mellow And I want to
feel like a queen Come below, I am keen
Fill my hollow.

One eye opens as the other one shuts Is this a distorted reality or just
purity?
I'm in limbo, a state of half-awakened sleep,
A confused arousal, it's all very threatening I wasn't prepared.

Learning

What you heard in my voice
Was jumping dragon flies in my soul
Wish I had the magic lantern to keep your light Instead I am the stone in
your stitched pocket
Condensed - quiet - still - unformed - softened by your glow
I have no sharp edges
And no words of my own – *abhasa* Maybe just a perception…of infinite
pain

Desert rose.

I am perplexed
Fuelled by neither lust nor desire

Our connection unexplained
Colliding against a sheer wall and a closed door I travel through words
Journey through paintings…drawings
The flow of unconsciousness…my inner knowing Butterflies in my
belly, I let down my hair
The door opens
I have never been so cold.

April

Early hours of an April morning

> I felt stripped of
> A promised kiss A vow for a dance
> A moment of passion.

Thoughts Over a Coffee Cup

I am touching your heartbeat It's layered with stories

I want to uncover unknown… Get to the core
I should have kept my hand for more It may have explained
Why I only feel your spiritual embrace And not your sexual chase

Touch my heart Now hold me again.

The End

Do you miss me
Or you still want to sting me
    and die?
Tick-tock, tick-tock Another one bites the dust For eventually we all must.

Gales

I twist and I turn Not wanting to burn
Yet I desire your touch

Lay on top of me
Cover me like a blanket of sand I want to feel the heat
　　of all the weight you carry
Burdens and joys

Connect with me as we climax
　　one of many.

Happy and content with a little lament Life is a bit tough
And sometimes makes me rough It's not my intent
But nobody asked for my consent.

You are not my soulmate Although you mate my soul I have told you this before But then you always go

Our paths will cross again
    under different stars and better times
There is no death, just growth
    until we learn

You are a big piece
Of my many previous altered lives

You have always been blue.

Reflecting on our yesterday Imagining a getaway

one dance…one kiss…

A feeling to reminisce.

Let's imagine There was no sin
Would I be your yin?

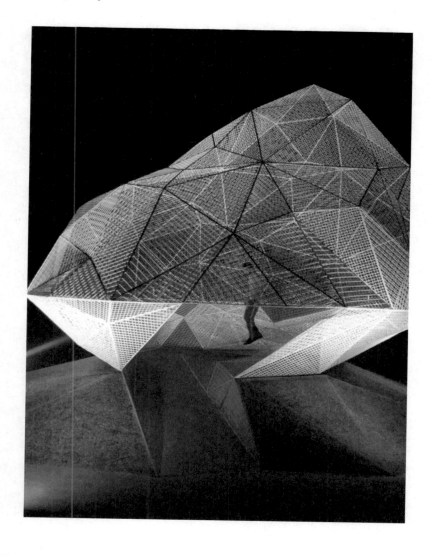

My Third Eye Is Blue

It's not on my forehead It's my nucleus
near my clitoris
I's always the thing that remains unsaid But you don't have a clue
As it is dubious when I am with you

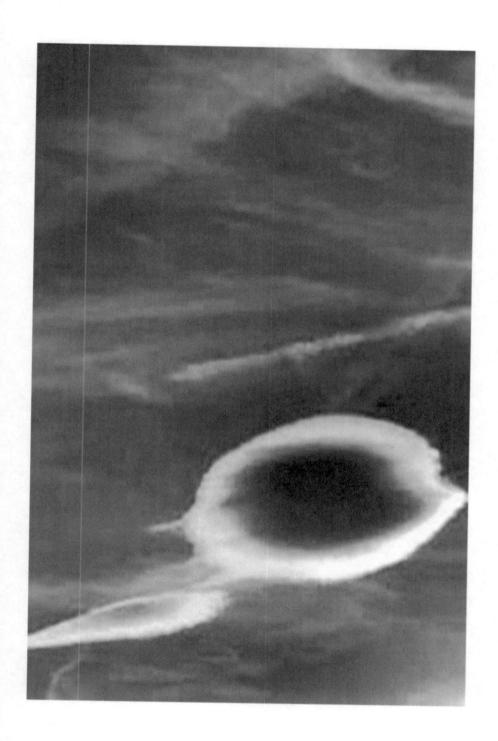

Your Words Offer Me Tranquillity

Your sweet-smelling sweat comforts me I will swim in this mystery, mine, yours,

Why? Because in this world, you advance me with guidance I understand through your eyes

Taste pleasure from your lips Once upon a time…

Your words offered me tranquillity, your embrace certainty Your lips pleasure, once upon a time.

Demons

God Truth Life Passion

words in my head

I want to touch them, push them Live them, explore
Discover beyond my barbed wire wall I want answers
Instead I hear hounding silence with no guidance

Another word: Compassion 171,000 words reduced to one: Your
name...

embedded in blue.

My Life Hangs on a Wall for All to See

In you I saw my love of art personified
My appreciation of the written word realized My love for music intensified

And then I became blind.

I Remember Our Fiery Kisses

They speak reflections
A breath of hope and sorrow An unknown tomorrow

Do I know you from before? A search for truth
Bring your pen and draw

Can you smell the sweet innocence of youth?

We Worship the Same Things

You and I…
The Sacred word
And the love we treasure in this world

You and I
The same mould
Hiding away from the cold

The World Threw Things at Me

Some moments were colored, some were dark Others were like the
agony of a Rubik's Cube,
I rotate it left and right to solve the riddle
    a waste of time – any empty ride
    I know the answer lies within my hands,

When the world is unkind
    I will choose the beauty of blue

                                                    It is you.

I Let Love In

My heart had no choice
    A cluster of emotions is compartments, Another addition, another
stain,

Why do I need this pain?
As if it is a necessary assignment the love
    the collapsing the healing
    the love
    the learning

    A fierce valve running on an ecclesiastical rhythm Take a deep slow
breath
    and many more
    there is strength in abundance I want tender love, I let love in again
    this time it is in blue.

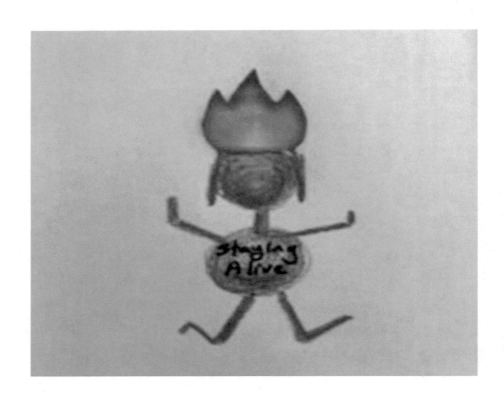

I read your messages through raindrops and sunshine
I decipher the clouds, a white one reads: Thinking of you
While the sunset always translates as I miss you

Then a whole different scenario takes over
And I wait for tomorrow

I saw your pure heart
And talked to your sad eyes,
They answered back Or was it that they spoke first?
That doesn't matter anymore
Pleasure wasn't the goal
I sent you away, do you remember the day?

I don't build walls,
I build on compassion
I think of you often – Never Naked
I feel you as a heavenly spirit and being with you is licit
Many thoughts remain unexpressed,

Can I float on your blue water and take a rest?

Passion Meets Me at Sea

Blue greets me
There are no walls here Just waves, joy and pain
And a window that frames your face Both beautiful
Swim with me in the deep end
What we have is something I cannot comprehend.

My story with Blue…my story with you.